The Cover Up

My Story of Other's Perceptions
Vs.
My Reality

Jo Anna B. Thomas

ISBN: 978-0-692-80501-5

The Cover Up

Proudly self-published through Divine Legacy Publishing, www.divinelegacypublishing.com

Dedicated to the memory of my Mother,
Elenor Joyce Jarrett Bowen

THE COVER UP

When you want to hide something, you cover it up. Depending on if you don't want to expose a cut or wound, you use a Band-Aid to let it heal. Essentially people are conditioned to find layers of protection and things that modify their wounds to achieve self-love and happiness. The problem arises when people no longer fit comfortably with the cover ups and no longer form fit into the mold that they once desired.

This book was written to help individuals become self-aware of their desire to cover up so that they can learn to love themselves as they are and embrace their inner and outer self. As my son says, "U gotta love yourself".

Hiding from your past and present will never allow you to fully love yourself and embrace your God-given talents. This book is intended to use my life story as an example of how not to hide and cover up from reality.

It is a motivational story of my life adventures from my childhood until now, in my mid 30's. In this book I get to let it all out from my rocky childhood, rushed adulthood, minority education, and name brand career.

I am finally ready to share my story of depression, self-hate, and my willingness to fight for a prosperous and rewarding life. As I spent years using external covers to hide my issues and pain, I am now ready to use my success and failures to motivate others to do better and go further. I have a long life to live and will do so by being myself with no cover ups. This is what some may label unapologetically being myself.

I also would love for urban youth to read my book and use it as a template to spread my message of endurance and preservation. Just because you grow up without money, materials, and emotional support doesn't mean you cant make it and develop your own prosperous life. I want the next generation to know that it's okay to leave their poor environments to better themselves educationally but always remember where they come from and lend a helping hand to uplift the future. In this world all you have is faith in God's plan for you.

FORWARD

From the outside you will be judged, but on the inside the truth flourishes.

People have always said the following: You always look nice. Your hair is pretty. Oh, your shoes are banging. You are smart. What school did you go to again? I want to be like you. How did you get to where you are at? You need to share your story.

Now it's time to tell my story. It's time to share how I mastered the art of covering up who I was inside to allow people to accept me for the things they saw on the outside.

I am more than just a pretty face. I am a torn and scarred woman. Over my life I have felt hurt and pain from parents, family, friends, jobs, relationships, and my own insecurities and fear. I have been afraid to be myself for so long. I have been afraid for people to see all the flaws in me. I am scared of who I have become at this point, and its time to make a change. I am nervous, but my fear does not stop me from taking chances and walking out on faith.

For many years I have lived behind my external characteristics. I sheltered myself with things that were appeasing to others. I wrote this book to heal and begin my new life. I will never regret the experiences that I had or the lessons that I learned, but from this point, I want to move forward and flourish in God's promise. May my story be an inspiration and a platform for me to share my successes and lessons learned with others.

Listen Up! I told my son that he had a voice and it must be heard, but I struggled for years using my voice. I was loud, and probably obnoxious, about a lot of things only as a cover up to my real voice. My voice of pain, sorrow, and hurt. Now it's my time to speak up for myself, fight for what's right for me, change the things that I can in my life, and continue to help motivate others with my story.

I have always wanted to write a motivational book, to tell my story, and even speak to people about my life. I put this dream on the back burner as I became accustomed to chasing a check in Corporate America and waiting on my personal life to grant me happiness. Now it's time for me to step out on faith and re-introduce myself to the world fully exposed.

HIDDEN CHILDHOOD

I don't remember much about my early childhood, but I do remember having everything I could imagine. I was born on June 1, 1980 to John B. Bowen and Eleanor Jarrett Bowen. We lived in a moderate triple-level story home in Markham, IL; also known as the south suburbs of Chicago. The house sat on a corner lot, with a huge back yard. I can remember the flowers my mom planted and the house and yard. I still think of the tree house that my dad built for my brother and I. It was our own play area with a swing that overlooked to yard. We weren't allowed to go outside and play alone, so it was a treat when our cousins and my mom's friends with children came over to play with us in our tree house.

My brother and I attended a daycare called Prince and Princess Daycare on Dixie Highway. I remember the work being too easy but the food was so good. All I wanted was the cheese substitute boxed macaroni and cheese with canned green beans. I don't know why I thought this toxic combination was so good.

House parties were amazing at my first house. I remember my mom and dad having company over after church. My mom would cook and have a pound cake ready every Sunday. I thought my house was huge. It was an average three bedroom suburban home with a huge side lot where my 3rd birthday party was held. Everyone came to my party; even my grandparents drove in from the city. I was super excited, and I remember the day being all about me. There was plenty of food, music, games, and even a pig roasting in the ground. My hair was braided with beads, and I had on my favorite pink jacket. My brother and I ran around playing awaiting the arrival of our favorite cousins.

I was literally a princess, and no one could tell me different. One day my fairytale life turned into a nightmare. I faintly remember my parents arguing. Movers where there and a lot of packing. That night we left the pretty house with flowers and headed to the big city of Chicago. This night changed my life forever.

I learned from my uncle, dad's brother, that my father had the largest black-owned roofing company in the 70's and early 80's. Successful, right? Something to be proud of, right? Well, hell no. It was more like this man had money and my mommy struggled, working numerous jobs and on was on welfare to make a way for my brother and I until she got sick. WTF! Yeah, I never understood how my dad could choose someone other than my mother, brother, and I.

Later, I learned that my dad had moved on and began another family leaving my mom, brother, and I all alone with no money and literally nothing. She could no longer afford the mortgage and had to move back home with her parents. At the time I didn't understand why he could not help us. Why didn't he love us anymore? What type of man lets the mother of his children suffer and struggle to take care of his reproductions?

My relationship with my dad didn't rekindle until my late teenage years while I was a freshman in college. I sought him and my half siblings. He never desired to have a relationship with me or my brother. This taught me to never chase a man because the first man I yearned for never pursued me or accepted me. Talk about daddy issues. Yeah, I have them. In short, he had his own psychotic issues that he needed to deal with. He learned from his mistakes and eventually apologized for not being there for me.

My childhood memories of my dad:

- random visits.
- he made promises and always broke them.
- he rarely called.
- he only answered for my grandfather as he wanted payment for roof repairs. In other words he only answered if he could make some money.

Despite his absence, I learned to love him for who he is and not to hold grudges. His absenteeism made me super strong but also has never allowed me to feel the real love of a man. I searched for love and my father's replacement via my grandfather, godfathers in and outside of the church, bosses, teachers, and eventually boyfriends. I never found the love I needed from a father.

Eventually, I learned that my father suffers from depression relating back to his childhood and relationship with his mother. So, end result: His mommy issues gave me daddy issues, facts. Some people know how to take bad situations and turn them into positive inspirations. My father did not; because of his parents he developed an immunity to responsibility. Given his failed marriage with my mother, he walked away, shut down, and did not live up to his obligations as a parent and father.

Once I pushed the relationship with my father, I learned that my father has always loved me. He always made a way to pop up for random life events. His internal struggle with happiness and not knowing how to handle his mistakes kept him from being a good father. Today I understand him because I have accepted the things that I cannot change, and I have broadened my understanding of life. I love him unconditionally because he is my earthly father and God put him in my life for many reasons.

By having an absent father, I constantly desire to want, have, and do more. I sought to find an understanding and answer to all of my questions, yet I found peace with my childhood and my life. Without my adversity and trials, I wouldn't have an inspirational story to tell. I learned how to take these negative moments in my childhood and develop them into a foundation for which my strength lies.

Life Lessons:

Learn to forgive so that life can go on. I did not have the best family structure as a child, but I haven't let it stop me. Of course I want a better life for my child. This has made me brutally honest with him about everything in my life, good or bad. I want him to learn from my mistakes. I call them daily life lessons. It strengthens me as I deal with my issues, and it shows him that I am not perfect but I work through my problems. I tell him to take this life skill and do better than me; be better than me.

Moreover, I have learned that it's God's plan and not my plan. I stay prayed up and focused on my passion and destiny set by God. This is what I call when God gives me the move forward plan and I am marching on his accord.

FAMILY LEGACY

Growing up a legacy within the Jarrett bloodline came with benefits and challenging detriments as well. We lived at 7000 S. Constance, which was a mini-mansion on the outside but a house of terror on the inside. During my parents divorce we moved from the suburbs of Chicago to the inner city with my grandparents. Well, actually my uncle Kenneth bought the house for my grandmother, but he exclaimed that is was his house and he set the rules.

My grandparents were both from Alabama. My grandfather traveled to Chicago for work then sent for my grandmother. At that time they only had two children: My eldest uncle Rod and my Mom, Baby Joyce. Their marriage struggled when they were younger and my grandma had a hard time raising their children, but all that mattered to me as that they were both in my life.

Their relationship was a bit weird. I never saw them kiss or hug until their end of life days. My granddaddy basically lived at his grocery stores in a loft style room he built above the store. The saying goes that you will be a better grandparent than you are parent, and they definitely lived up to it.

My granny was the best! She taught me how to cook, clean, and most importantly count money. Yes, I said count money. My granny was responsible for keeping up with my granddaddy's money. I'll explain more later. She always referred to my brother and I as "the children." She loved us so much; she always cared about us and helped make sure we had what we needed, not wanted. One time my grandfather bought me my first pair of Michael Jordan's, the ones with the wings. OMG. I was so excited. She was so mad at my grandfather that she fussed at him so. Granny never cursed but could tell you a thing or two in very few words. She was more forward looking and thought he should have been saving the money for my future education. She was correct.

My grandfather was an Old G. He was never affiliated with a gang, neither a pimp, nor a hustler. He was what you would call a "cool cat". Everyone that knew and met him respected him. He called all the shots, and people would listen and do as he said. He was a pioneer businessman in the Black community. He believed in black businesses and helping the community. From what I heard, he wasn't the best father or husband but in my eyes he was my dad. I learned a lot from him. I watched him run his business, interact with salesmen, conduct financial business at the bank, and deal with customers directly. As I grew up, my respect and admiration for him grew immensely. Oh, did I mention he didn't even have an eighth grade education? Yup, pure genius. He inspired my pursuit for education and even my career.

The house we lived in had four massive bedrooms, kitchen, dining room, living room, and even its own library. There was also a backyard and my grandma's private garden that was just as big as the house. I may have been sad about leaving our nice suburban house and not seeing my dad, but I was happy to be around my grandparents and family.

Just when I thought we were going to be living good, I really got to know my aunt and uncles. It was the fall of 1984. I remember being in kindergarten when my world began to change.

My eldest uncle was a paranoid schizophrenic. He served in Vietnam, and my mom said when he returned home he was never the same. On top of his psychological issues he was a flamboyant homosexual. My mother taught my brother and I early about sex, sexual orientation, and gender roles. She wanted us to be informed about our new environment to say the least. My mother often recalls her brother being sick way before the military. She then goes on to tell me countless stories about their traumatic childhood growing up a Jarrett.

My aunt was the coolest person I know to this date. She always had a sharp leather jacket, cowboy boots, and a leather cap. She rocked it. Later I learned she was a lesbian and wanted to be a boy. I didn't care; l loved my Tia. She was fun and outgoing. She played with us, wrestled, picked us up from school, and even tried to teach us Spanish. When my mom was too afraid to teach me how to drive, she did and even would loan me her 2-door Ford explorer during high school. She was equally as nice to my brother. On most days she stayed high. She was an open lesbian and feminist to the extreme. I often wanted her to like men, get married, and have children so that I could have first cousins.

My aunt's style and bad habits didn't bother me too much. I just wanted her to stop because I saw what it was doing to my grandmother. I knew she stole money and items from the stores and house. I used to find her pipes and throw them away. I even saw her smoking a few times and would grab the pipe from her. I just couldn't understand why she needed to get high. To this day I still don't understand, but I pray for her inner peace and healing. Maybe this was because of her childhood as well.

My other uncle was never home. My grandparents owned several food and liquors stores, a restaurant, and a lounge. He basically lived at one of the stores like my granddad. My mom would take us to visit him on 63rd and Cottage, the location of Jarrett's food and liquor store and Marvin's Onyx super-club. He would be so happy to see my brother and I. We would run in the store and everyone would greet us with excitement. Some of the workers threw shade because they thought we were rich spoiled kids, but they never could understand our struggle. This uncle was not so much openly gay, but we knew he had a boyfriend that he employed in the stores. Things got tough when his boyfriend died at an early age from AIDS, then my uncle died the summer of 1997. Before his death my uncle became very angry and bitter as if he knew he was going to die, so he took his anger out on my brother and I.

Communication in this household was rough to say the least. My aunts, uncles, as well as my granddad didn't communicate well at all. They cursed, hollered, and fought each other constantly to express their frustrations and problems. I must admit I did inherit a potty mouth and aggressive tendency growing up around this. I am learning not to use voice words to express myself when I get super mad, instead of flying off the gasket like my family taught me. I'm still a work in process, so I have learned to avoid negative situations and walk away when I can. I don't like that side of me at all.

I had to learn how to express myself. Sometimes I hid in the house crying, but I turned those tears into reading and learning from my uncle's books in the family's library. Yes, the house had a library. He was super crazy yet super smart, so he bought all kinds of texts books. From grammar-school to college. I buried myself in the books to escape my surroundings.

My grandmother always told me loose lips sinks ship, and I finally realize what she was saying. Now I think before I speak and I say things with the same passion, but I use my extended vocabulary to express myself while keeping it simple and plain.

The family dynamics and my wealthy grandparents enabled drug addiction, alcoholism, and overall abuse. I never knew what my mom meant by this until I got old enough to understand and see my grandparents hurt and mistreated over these addictions, and that showed me the truth about people and life.

With all of this chaos I began to look at my family differently and wondered if other families where like this. I longed for my own family. I wanted it to be different, full of love and support. Not sure if I should have been looking for this outside of myself. It seems too perfect and perfect does not exist anywhere but in Christ.

My mother was what we call the black sheep in a dysfunctional family. She was different as the only child to marry and produce offspring of her own. My mom labeled them the Adams family, as in the television show. She exclaimed that each person had their own distinct TV character but only in real life. My mom was far from perfect. She smoked weed, even sold some to help pay the bills. She would drink to kill her sorrow and pain, which I learned later on was depression. She never abused us, she never neglected us, and she gave us her all. I would always fuss at her about smoking cigarettes and weed in front of my brother and I when we were children. I began to immolate the environment that I was raised around. I hollered and I cursed at her. Yes, I did. I didn't know how to let my mom know that I didn't like what she was doing in any other way. This caused major problems between us because I was very disrespectful, but I was a child that had a voice and no one to talk to.

Over my teenage years we mended our relationship to get along because I adored my mother and she loved me unconditionally. She wanted the best for me, and I wanted the best for her. My mother now suffers from lung, heart, and vascular issues due to smoking. She eventually told me that she started smoking cigarettes as a 12-year-old child to calm her nerves as she was raised in a similar chaotic environment as a child. At this point I vowed to change my ways and become a better person. To this day I have open candid discussions with my child and try to teach him from my mistakes as I fight for this cycle to end.

I speak more about my maternal family as I was raised around them. My paternal family is equally, if not more, dysfunctional. Mental health, drugs, and alcohol

12

abuse are real problems within our families and communities. Let's not hold it in, no more cover ups, it's time to talk about it and support each other. Let's band together, pray, and get the professional help that we need to end this vicious cycle.

Life Lessons:

You can make it out. No matter what your surroundings may be. I'm not saying it's easy, but it is a positive way out. Even if no one is telling you can make it, tell yourself that you can. Keep saying it, write it down, and read it over and over again. Set a goal, find a dream, and stay focused on it. Pray Pray Pray. Ask God for guidance

Although my surroundings warranted a negative outcome for my future, I was taught so much. Growing up a Jarrett was not easy, but I took away the good.

- Entrepreneurship - I am a think tank. My brain is constantly churning thinking of new ideas and analyzing various things as I look for synergies and connections.

- Business Acumen - My grandfather always said, "I ain't no damn fool". Well, no I'm not. I have been exposed to a lot of business models and organizations, so I do have a strong voice for those that want to listen.

- Leadership - I can't follow a dummy.

- Fearlessness - I fear no one or anything but God, so I am always testing the waters, exploring, and challenging myself to be better ever day.

- Tenacity - I will not give up. I will figure it out. I may take a heavy blow, but I will surely rebound for victory.

The moral of the story: Heroes make lemonade out of lemons then turn it into country time lemonade. It's never easy, but you will be rewarded with peace and overall happiness.

SCHOOL YEARS

Point blank period, I loved school. I was a classic "nerd" and I was proud of it. I still enjoy the educational learning opportunities in life versus worldly things. Reading, writing, and doing math gave me an escape from my reality. I ran straight home from school each day to do my homework. The library in my grandparents' house had bookcases built into the walls that housed great books, encyclopedias, and magazines. My uncle Rod was an editor after he was honorably discharged from the Army post Vietnam. He suffered from paranoia and deep mental illness. Uncle Rod was highly educated and loved to read. Some of the books were not appropriate for children, but I enjoyed the Child Craft books where I read about different topics from A to Z.

During my grammar school years, my mom went back to school to obtain her GED. I was about ten years old when she completed the night and evening program at the neighborhood institute. She worked during the day and attended school at night and on the weekends. I started to miss her dearly, so I would hop a ride with my grandfather's driver to the store in which she worked and when I got old enough I caught the bus or walked to her jobs. I wanted to see my momma. I attended weekend classes with her and even helped her with her homework. Mom showed me to never give up and to work hard. Despite the challenges from her past she woke up every day to be the best mom she could be and provide for her children.

Mom kept working and attended junior college until my brother and I entered high school. She began to work multiple jobs to meet her children's increasing needs as teenagers. Going to high school in Chicago is very similar to attending a historically black college or university. As the city is very segregated, you are always surrounded predominately by other black boys and girls while in school. Instead of sororities and fraternities, there are female and male cliques along with city gangs. The cliques are divided amongst the good and bad and moreover the rich vs the poor. I was super small in high school as I only stood 4'11" and weighed about 100lbs. Shorty and Lil Bit were my grammar school and high school nicknames. I was branded due to my size. At first I didn't like it, but I figured that it wasn't so bad. Others usually picked on you for some type of physical attribute so ignore and embrace the label I thought to myself. At least they weren't calling me ugly or fat. Being a kid can be rough, especially in those middle school and high school years. Are you noticing my cover up?

Can you see how I started off my life hiding and avoiding?

Living in a grey area of life, I was an academic-focused individual that could be considered a nerd, but I also participated in a popular clique as a cheerleader. I was fortunate not to get involved in too many conflicts in school. I had a few arguments here and there and even got into a fist fight with a dear friend from which we reconciled and remain good sister friends to this day. I tried to stay pretty neutral and associated with all different types of personalities while in high school. I wanted to be well rounded and explore other areas of interest as I continued to play the clarinet in the high school marching and concert band. I was always told by teachers, counselors, and mentors to be very active in high school to increase my likelihood of being admitted to the college or university of my choice and receive more scholarships.

Growing up I never thought forward enough to pick a career or think of what college I wanted to go to. I just knew that in order to get away from home and my family, I needed knowledge and a good job. In order not to struggle like my mother raising two children as a single parent, I needed to get more than a high school education. My mom did not finish high school because she ran away from home and got married early. She exclaims she wanted to get away from the craziness and drama that surrounded her. As I was raised around the same family members and a second generation coupled with alcohol and the introduction of a new drug, crack, I didn't blame her. I wanted out myself. Not from her but from the vicious cycle that I recognized at an early age. This is why I hit the books, studied hard, and found opportunities to nurture me positively and academically.

Getting good grades also paid in my family. My grandparents were very adamant about my brother and I doing well in school. They would give us $10-20 for getting A's, so I worked hard to get that easy money. Too bad they did not teach me how to effectively manage my money and live within my means. I learned from what I saw. We had a lot of money and we spent a lot of money.

Life Lessons:

Although at a young age in grammar and high-school you think other students' and children's opinions are important as you make new friends and assimilate to the surrounding cultures, I believe that defining yourself and happiness should be the priority. I hate to say it, but these people really don't matter. They are temporary obstacles that you must navigate to get to the next level in life. You will grow up and surround yourself with people that mutually love and care about you.

Everyone's childhood is different and that is what makes us the individuals that we are. During childhood it may seem that others may have more or less than you, but it really doesn't matter. The future is determined by your faith and self-commitment. Never let your shortcomings limit you and never allow your valuables to define you.

This is probably the shortest chapter in the book intentionally. No, I don't have anything to hide. The point is that I believe childhood schoolmates are not that significant unless you are cut from the same cloth, meaning you share the same morals and ethics. If they are your true friends, they will stick around through thick and thin. If not they will eventually disappear.

COLLEGE BLISS

I needed a way out from my dysfunctional home environment. Even in our new townhouse, I wasn't comfortable. I wanted to so much more for my life. I dreamed of living where there was peace and happiness. I wanted to see the moon and stars at night, run through the neighborhood, and even take time to stop and smell the roses. I often dreamt of living in sunny California. I always saw the movies and articles about how the movie stars lived, and I imagined that it could be me one day. I was definitely an out of the box dreamer. My childhood Amtrak train ride from Chicago to Los Angeles sealed the deal of my California Dreams.

I decided to go away to college to get away from my home environment. Yeah, I can feed you the fluff about getting a stellar education and good job, but this book is about being honest and I just wanted to be at peace. I endured emotional stress and developed anxiety while growing up in a dysfunctional family and environment.

I also I wanted to be different. I never really fit in with the kids in high school. I mean, we were all cool but I didn't feel the organic connection I was looking for. I decided to experiment, be different, and attend the University of Notre Dame while most of my high school classmates chose state universities and HBCUs.

When I got to Notre Dame, I really didn't fit in as I expected. I was out of my element. I am a Black girl from the south-side of Chicago, damnit! This lily white university was nothin' I was used to. I wasn't an athlete. My family had lost all of their wealth to drugs and bad financial management, so I was relatively poor in comparison to my classmates.

I was one of I believe two Black girls in my dorm. During my college years from, 1997-2001, Black Girl Magic was not celebrated as it is today. Having curves in all the right places was not popular back then and moreover the classic "Susie" and "Becky" were not trying to be your best friend or even associate. The white girls were either rich or sheltered. Most never had interaction with a Black girl in their entire lives.

Taking showers and personal grooming was always questioned by the white girls. They asked questioned like: "Why do you put oil on your hair? Why do you wear hair scarfs and bonnets? What type of soap do you use? Having nappy hair was not celebrated or embraced, so I permed my hair so even more questions were asked.

I was accustomed to having Sunday dinners with my mom, brother, grandparents, uncles, and aunt as we dined eating good soul food prepared with love. I wanted a good old fashion meal without using the common kitchen and being starred at and judged for my collard greens and fried chicken fetish. They probably were just as hungry as I was now that I reflect back. Now these traditional Black Sunday dinners are a delicacy and sold in gentrified neighborhoods at astronomical prices. I should have cooked and charged for plates and saved that money earned. What I should have done differently can be another book, but self-reflection is extremely important. Eventually, I moved off campus to a 1 bedroom apartment in which I remained until graduation. I could no longer take the questions about my hair, when do I wash it, why do I perm it, etc.

College became a blur when my mom got sick during my sophomore year. She was diagnosed with an Aortic Aneurism. She had to stop working, and her health took a toll. By my junior year her doctors recommended a surgery to replace a part of her Aorta. Yes, I said that correctly. The heart surgeons at the University of Chicago wanted to replace the a portion of the main valve of my mother's heart. I was attending the University of Notre Dame. I worked hard to be admitted to this university, and I couldn't drop out and leave a goal unfinished or claim defeat. There were already so many odds against me as a black woman at a majority university studying under the difficult Finance and Economics major. I told my professors and academic dean the situation with my mom, and I left school to attend to her hospital bedside. Everyone was understanding about my family situation. My professors allowed me to miss class and turn in my work late. I got a chance to go be with my mom during that difficult time.

At that point I knew why I chose ND. Although I never felt the initial fit, this was my family and they supported me and wanted to see me succeed. My mom got better, and I went back to school full time. I mean, I never un-enrolled; I was just around campus more and attended all of my classes. Before the surgery mom even came to stay with me in my dorm room and afterwards my apartment so that I wouldn't worry about her health as I was away from her at school. She got to know some of my friends, counselors, and professors very well. Mom always supported my goals and helped me fulfill each one with her love and blessings.

In college I served in multiples roles as a natural leader organizing events and helping redefine students clubs and groups on campus. I was a peer mentor and coach as others always came to my apartment for refuge as we engaged in my heartfelt talks. In our discussions we identified problems and developed solutions with plans for success. I was even a stylist as I coordinated outfits and assisted with hairstyles to help my friends maintain their self-esteem through adequate grooming and self-confident physical presentation. My apartment was like your big mama's or grandma's house where there was always food and love. Each year new Black students would come to the house with groceries and special requests for my soul food.

Because of my hard work and dedication, I graduated on time with a BBA in Finance and Business Economics as well as a minor in Computer Applications. I felt damn good. I had accomplished one of my biggest dreams and goals. I had made it! So I thought, at this point. Little did I know life had so much more to teach me.

My only regret was not taking the time to find me. My complete college career revolved around my football boyfriend and my mom. I didn't know who I really was outside of a girlfriend and daughter. I mean, I had an employable major and got good internships during the summer, but soon I learned that I wasn't in love with what I was doing or myself.

Life Lessons:

Graduating was not a cover up! It was a legitimate goal that set me up for life and opened so many doors for me. I encourage all young people to go to college, explore their dreams, and find the ultimate passion to pursue so that they will never have to work a day in their life.

Step out of your comfort zone. It's a big world out there and, in order to compete, you need exposure. I am NOT saying lose yourself or hide from your culture, but it's okay to expand your knowledge base and interact with different races and cultures. It will only make you more powerful and successful in what you chose to do.

A soul mate, boo, bae, and love of your life will be sent to you by God. Don't rush it; enjoy college. Study abroad, travel, and enjoy college life. Define who you are before you allow a relationship to define you.

CORPORATE
STRUGGLE

Soon after Notre Dame, both of my grandparents died. My eyes began to open and I knew I had to make a way for my mother and I. With her aneurism, multiple surgeries, and chronic illness I became overly focused on her and my career.

I wore high heels, suit or dress, and carried the LV briefcase. I walked with a stride that caught the attention of all that I passed. I led meetings in front of top executives reviewing financials and even gave updates on critical programs and project plans. I was known for my agility and dexterity with the ability to solve complex problems and deal with difficult people/teams all while accomplishing the set goal. I was called a super star and was highly sought out for my unique and diverse skill set as a financial/business analyst and project management professional. I thought I was the shit! I looked good, I felt good, and I was paid good.

I hate to say this, but I forgot I was Black. I mean, I had a remarkable education from Notre Dame and then early in my career I obtained my MBA from Northwestern University Kellogg School of Management. With experience and a kick ass education, I just knew I was the shit and ready to conquer corporate America. In my mind color didn't matter anymore. Oh, how was I wrong and completely covering up. I figured if I worked hard I would be promoted, make more money, and begin to solve all my problems. NOT!!!

Don't get me wrong, I never forgot my roots, but I didn't understand why I had to work so hard and why others who did significantly less than me climbed the corporate later with ease. This is what we call the "Black Tax". I mean, it took the best of me. I was stuck beneath the glass ceiling, and I was fed up. Given my strong personality and vast communication skills, I did not hide what I was feeling. I tried to play the game and navigate the waters to get where I wanted to be, but I was not successful. I was constantly given excuses on why I could not do something.

I even had managers that focused on my physical attributes such as my hair and clothes. One even questioned my ability to have time for date night with my hubby. SO unprofessional. At this point, I realized that corporate was draining me mentally and spiritually. I was fed up with the corporate game. I didn't want to play it anymore.

We say God works in mysterious ways. Soon I began experiencing pain in my hands, arms, and neck. I learned that I have Degenerative Disc Disease caused by repetitive stress injury. Yes, typing and working my ass off jacked me up. Or as I'd rather say, God revealed his plan for me.

After over 2 years of with struggling with my health, fighting through daily chronic pain, and legal issues, I decided to focus on rebuilding myself and opening my eyes to what God wanted me to see.

On May 12, 2014, I lost it all.

Starting from the beginning, I always wanted to be a businesswoman. Growing up watching my family conduct business as "Bosses" inspired me to be a leader in the business world. It was like I grew up as an apprentice to business. As mentioned, in my childhood I was trained to be an entrepreneur, but my family pushed me to get an education and work in the larger business world. My grandparents thought college would be best for me since they didn't complete grammar school. I was not the first generation college student in my family, but they wanted me to be well educated. On some days I agree with their push but on some days I don't.

In my corporate career, I would land the "great job" at the perfect company, but I was not challenged or fulfilled. I would master the position, innovate and improve the process, but still felt empty. Sometimes I would get a "job well done" or petty cash bonus, but I was never rightfully promoted or moved to a desirable position. Being the outspoken person that I am, yes, I asked why in so many politically correct and straightforward ways. You know it, I got the classic bullshit responses, so I paved my own career path searching for something that just wasn't in Corporate America but lived deep in my core.

Yes, the glass ceiling was all too real for me. I worked for outstanding organizations, but I wasn't going to play the corporate game or be the "house negro" from slavery. I was rarely celebrated or rewarded for my superior work or innovative contributions. I was pigeon holed and forced to continue to support middle management initiatives without the recognition or promotions.

To make a long story short, corporate almost killed me! I was overworked, stressed, and developing medical problems that I didn't even know existed. I made a lot of money but was still underpaid as a young black female compared to my white male counterparts. It took a life altering illness to stop me from giving my all to corporate and start investing in myself. This is not to bash organizations but shed light on how individuals need to perform jobs that pay their heart and soul and the let the financial benefits manifest while fulfilling your God-given purpose.

Life Lessons:

As a young professional I loved the titles, cash, benefits, and perks of working in Corporate America. I should have saved more cash, but this isn't a book about financial management. My point is that I should have used corporate as a stepping stone to fund my real goals. I should have pursued my consulting and motivational endeavors early on in my career. I should have made my life the priority and not the corporate agenda.

My advice would be to use corporate or any non-entrepreneurial work experience for just what it is: the experience. Take that knowledge and move on. Build the skill set and toolkit to create the job of your dreams and never work the rest of your life.

I have learned to take breaks to regroup, sharpen the saw, and rear myself to handle the lemons that arise in my life. Unfortunately, while taking my breaks, my mind is so free and clear that I begin to mentally brainstorm, think, and come up with marvelous ideas and plans to do bigger and better things. I'm still working on actually freeing my mind and relaxing. Don't judge me. I am aware and working on it.

It's okay to take a break to find yourself. You don't owe anybody any explanation for when you need a break or when to take the break. Don't let society, family, and jobs define what you do day to day. Start your day and end your day the way you want. Life is too short to be so confined and rigid. Create a life full of fun and flexibility.

I'm not saying don't go to school or don't get a job, but I am saying don't forget to find balance and enjoy life. Remember life is short and you only have one chance to make the best of it.

"When I didn't like my job, I quit

When I wasn't happy with the person I was with, I left

When I wanted to travel, I did

You can't always wait for time to change things in your life, sometimes you have to change things yourself" - Anonymous

Change is OKAY! It's actually fun! People may call you inconsistent or a gypsy, but you must live for yourself!

LOVE AND LUST

As a child I would sing and write this song:

"Nobody loves me, nobody likes me, nobody cares".

I think all female children go through a period of where they feel alone, but I think I had it pretty bad. My mom worked all the time. My grandmother did not show much emotion, and only said to pray about it. I mean, I was lost looking for love and attention. I tried to bond with my girlfriends, but of course they had their own drama. I even tried to connect with other family members, but they only saw me as the spoiled little princess. They failed to realize my mom's struggle, which inevitably became my own struggle. It's funny how a pattern and legacy repeats itself.

I would cry myself to sleep at night because I felt so alone. My mom was stressed out from all the work, bills, and no help raising her children. My grandparents became distant, and my brother and I grew apart. I could not deal, so I decided to start paying more attention to the boys. Yes, it was about that time. I had my share of crushes and boys I liked throughout grammar school and even early in high school, but I never really cared about them. I was more interested in school and learning. I was very focused, because I had to be better and do better than my mom. I really wanted to make her and myself proud.

In college, I fell in love. I knew he was the one. I had a few bad break ups before him, but this time I was sure he would never leave me and I would never leave him. We were so close and connected; we told each other we were "one". I was the type of girl that did not get around much. If I was in love, I was in love and had my mind made up. The problem was he wasn't ready, but I was. Needless to say, our relationship ended soon after we both graduated from college. I had moved on to a love interest that started paying me attention. I was not ready to move on, but I had to mend my broken heart, or so I thought. I knew it this time. I was really in love. This time I wasn't waiting around, I spoke early about my goals and marriage. We fell in love and I thought we were on the same page with life. I learned later that he went along with me in order not to lose me. He wanted what I wanted but wasn't necessarily in a rush like me. Things happen, we had a baby, got married, and of course our marriage struggled for years. Countless attempts to fix things on both sides made us grow farther apart.

Looking back, I never took the time to heal from my college relationship. He's my college long-term boyfriend who played in the NFL. The distance ... I worked and he played ball ... I didn't follow him around the country. He knew I never got over him. My husband knew my love for this man, but at that point we had grown too far apart and my new guy paid more attention to my immediate needs.

I went back to singing my favorite song:

"Nobody loves me, nobody likes me, nobody cares"

Man, I was delusional, I was fine as wine. All the men wanted to holla, but I was stuck. I was never the type of girl to date around loosely. I wanted consistency. I wanted my own MAN. I was never big into sharing. This time I am looking at my past and learning more about myself. I finally figured out what makes me happy and what is takes to make another person happy.

Instead of finding that new love interest to make me forget about the past, I have invested more time into myself. I am focusing on future opportunities to develop and grow my consulting dreams as Network JO and the Being Basic JO Blog inspirational and motivational platform, and well as laying the educational and financial foundation for my son to drive and grow.

Don't get me wrong. I made a lot more LOVE mistakes than I detailed above, but I have learned to move beyond the love of a man to loving myself. When it's my time to enjoy love again, I pray that it's God sent and ordained. This time around it's finally about me owning who I am. I now understand that perfect relationships do not exist, but God has given me what I need and I chose not to question the continued blessings he will reveal.

I am so happy with myself. I have begun to travel to different countries by myself to relax and embrace the unconditional love that I have finally found in myself. I'm not saying it has been an easy road, but I know that with my faith in God and love for myself I can get through anything!

Today, I realized that I fight everyday to avoid depression and increase my self-esteem. I am a battered woman emotionally and physically. I now can admit I covered my pain, and I hid from my truth. Now I can work on myself as I have revealed who I am to myself, family, and now you.

Today, I will rebuild myself. I have my "Go Forward Plan". I no longer need my marriage or relationship to validate my existence as a woman. I am no longer ashamed of my mistakes as a woman and mother. I no longer need a title or position to define me. I am Jo Anna Boshana Bowen.

Life Lessons:

So my son has said it the best, "I got trust issues". Yes, I know you're thinking that he is a superstar and super smart. I tell you, you are reading my story. Wouldn't you have trust issues, too? Well, in order to move on you have to let some of the pain and hurt go. No matter how deep you are in a pity party, check yourself, find help, and live on.

Never marry looking for someone to love you more than you love yourself. Never expect things to change post marriage. Don't rush, take your time, and the right person will come into your life at the right time. Make sure you are equally yoked. Make sure you both are aligned on life goals and most importantly are God fearing and God worshiping servants of Christ.

Ponder this: "I'm finding that the men I'm physically attracted to do nothing for me mentally or emotionally while the men that have my mind blown over intellectual knowledge and dialect do nothing for me physically as the attraction is nowhere to be found. Do I settle or keep searching for the best of both worlds? Figure out what makes you the happiest and go for it" - JO

Moral of the story is that you must LOVE yourself first before you can show love to anyone else. Once you are in love with being you, then the external love will overflow and that soul mate will present themselves without any doubt. That love thing will manifest and flourish on the outside and inside.

EXPLORATION AND SEARCH

My mom coined me Dora from the children's show "Dora the explorer". Not only did I take my tour of corporate America across various industries, companies, and states, I also loved to travel to places with my son and even alone.

When I completed college, I was able to take my mom to the East Coast as I started my career. She was able to visit cities in New York, New Jersey, and Pennsylvania. She took road trips with me throughout Indiana and Ohio. She would even fly across the country to the state of Washington and California to spend months visiting and helping me raise my son. In reward for her unconditional love, we've vacationed in the Caribbean together where we let out hair down and enjoyed fun in the sun. I am so glad to have experienced such amazing time traveling with my mom.

Sometimes I would just want to escape my surroundings and reality. One day I FaceTimed my mother from Aruba. My son was actually with me and she yelped, "Where are you two?"

My son said, "Nanny, we are in Aruba."

Her response was exceptionally classic: "Your mom is Dora the Explorer and you are Diego." We all laughed and still laugh to this day.

I usually gave her a heads ups about where we were going and when we were coming back to ease her nerves, but that time I just up and left. I needed to feel the wind beneath my wings. Travel has always afforded me freedom while living in a confined world of work and adulthood responsibilities. To combat it, I took the boy with me as I figured motherhood can be done anywhere while we see the world.

I could not study abroad during high school because of limited funds and during college my mother was extremely ill. I always wanted to explore and learn but never had the ability. Traveling has always been a passion for me as I sought opportunities that allowed me to see new places and create new experiences. As a child, I only flew on an airplane to Alabama and rode a train to California, both from Chicago. These experiences allowed me to see that there was more out there in the world beyond the south side of Chicago.

My son and I have been traveling together since he was 6 weeks old. I got clearance from my OBGYN and we hit the airways. Our first stop was Disney World and Universal Studios in Orlando, FL. He was the perfect baby on the flight and in the parks. We walked off my pregnancy weight, and he soaked up the sunshine. I knew then we would always travel together and have fun. He will always be my favorite travel partner.

As my ex-husband and I separated, my son would venture back to Chicago from California to visit his father and other family members. I was not always able to travel with him, so he initiated flying alone at the age of seven. At first I was a nervous wreck, but he had an iPhone in hand and was so accustomed to flying he was unbothered. My lil man was learning how to be an independent man. From flying all those years with me, he had the routine down pat. He wasn't afraid, and it taught me not to be afraid as he was becoming ready for many adventures to come. I had taught him to take risks and explore just as I had ventured out in the world. I was so excited for his experiences, and I continued to let him fly alone when visiting his father. Once a helicopter mom, I had transitioned to a proud mom.

Over the years, despite my illness, I continued to travel. When my health limits me I find cool activities within my city to partake in and live an adventurous life. Sometimes it's just plain old fun being a tourist in my own city and revisiting places that make me smile and happy. There are seasonal events, outdoor concerts, and pop up bars that make me feel as though I'm somewhere different. The best part about it is that I feel free. All the life stresses disappear, and I am happy and at peace with myself.

I simply love to travel, and this past year I was able to take my son to China for educational and world life experiences. That trip was amazing. I didn't realize how much fun I would have just sitting back and watching my son explore a part of the world rich with culture and tradition. I booked the trip a year prior as a college friend hooked me up with a cheap travel opportunity. I had and entire year to acquire our visas and scrape together travel funds for daily spending. I was so glad that most of our meals were covered and we had an English-speaking tour guide. Her name is Fei Fei, and she is my Chinese best friend. I look forward to visiting China again and exploring the African pyramids.

This trip was almost canceled as I was dealing with my own health issues and the recent decline in my mother's health due to Lung Cancer and Coronary Artery Disease. My mother insisted on our pre-arranged travel and was able to stay strong in our absence. Upon our return, I had to place her on at home hospice care as she was no longer able to mobilize around her apartment alone. She was able to FaceTime us through the trip and even ride the bullet train with us. She saw one of the seventh wonders of the world, the Great Wall. I could not ask for a better time and the blessing of being able to virtually take my mother halfway around the globe. This is an experience that I am glad she was able to witness in her final days.

Life Lessons:

Travel/Explore: Don't be afraid to leave the hood. Don't be afraid to go places where no one or rather a few look like you. Take the opportunity to understand different cultures, not changing who you are but nurturing your soul and exposing yourself to the world. You only have one lifetime so you must value each day and seek opportunities to do fulfilling and positive things outside of your comfort zone.

Don't be afraid to travel alone. Sometimes company ruins your experience.

Learn: You will never know it all. Seek ways to build your knowledge on things that interest you. Keep building and looking for ways to turn your knowledge into a profit.

Live: Don't forget to live. No matter what you do for a day job even, if it's your passion, don't forget to take a break and live.

Don't model your time and location based on others. People will judge you whether you are near or far, so go ahead and live the best life you can possibly live while fulfilling all of your desires. Embrace change and learn how to mitigate risk, as life will throw you unanticipated surprises daily.

PEOPLE RELATIONSHIPS

This chapter of the book may get me into a lot of trouble with people that know me personally, but oh well. Let's us commence and keep it real. As a child my mom always said very bluntly, "Fuck a Friend". No filter used. Her father always told her that, "When you grow older you will be able to count your friends on one hand and have a lot of fingers left over," all while waving all five of his fingers at her. He also told his children and grandchildren that, "Your friend is in your pocket." He was referring to money, and now that I'm older his old sayings were very brutally honest and pure facts. The generational lessons continue as I tell my son the same. The moral is that people play various roles in your life during certain life circumstances. They are intended to be that friend at the point in time, and the relationship good or bad is not promised or necessarily needed for the future.

"Frenemy" is an oxymoron and a portmanteau of "friend" and "enemy" that can refer to either an enemy pretending to be a friend or someone who really is a friend but also a rival. According to Wikipedia, the term is used to describe personal, geopolitical, and commercial relationships both among individuals and groups or institutions.

I started to name this chapter Frenemy, but I changed it to people. Here is why: Usually your cousins are your first friends. Well, not for me. I was bullied by my cousins to do the things that they wanted me to do with them. I did things to please them, like not being myself. It was my only escape from home and my troubled surroundings. I just wanted to have fun and fit in. I loved to be with my cousins, but I always had to follow their agenda. I accepted it because I had no options and I didn't want to stay home.

As I grew older I realized the cousins that love and support me would just be around without me doing anything. Now, refer to most people as just people. I learned the hard way that family titles or length of friendship and even sharing significant experiences don't stop "people" from being "people".

Some people you can only do certain things with. I have been fortunate to have beautiful people in my life. Don't get me wrong, some were bad and mean, but I learned so many valuable lessons.

There are types of people that I have met in my life.

The Sista-friend:

- She calls everyday.
- She dries my tears.
- She has my best interest at heart.
- She claims to be my best friend.

The Soul Sister:
- Feels my pain and hurts when I hurt.
- Ride or die that is willing to take on risk with and without you.
- Supportive and will be there to the end.
- Available whether near or far.
- Time and distance does not stop this friendship or bond.

Frenemy:
- Keep her close and watch her.
- She always has something negative to say.
- She judges everything you do.
- She's simply petty, and she will never uplift you.
- Seems like all these women eventually end in this category.
- She will not help you if it will position you ahead of her.
- She will limit her love if she feels you are being loved too much by many.

Oh I must not forget, the Friend that brags about everything:

- Materials matter.

- Always on social media and snapping pictures for the 'gram.

- The new car, man, house, job, etc. It's all about the new new.

- She is self-consumed.

- She never asks about you and always talks about herself in each verb tense.

Let's stop it with the best friend title. What does that really mean? I just don't get how people harp on the bestie title so much. I thought I had best friends at different points in my life because I told them all of my personal business and they seemed to care about me, but I learned they just needed to hear something to make them forget about their own problems and issues. I was just being used as a pedestal so their problems could seem lighter than mine. I used the platform to release tension and stress. I should have invested in counseling instead. Either way, the talks helped as I wasn't holding things inside, but I could have gotten more structured therapy and even spiritual counseling to help me navigate through painful trying times.

When a person is down on their luck about their marriage, health, and financials, I don't want to hear about how good your life is. I don't want a pity party, but I don't want a slap in my face reminder about how fucked up my life is. Not to hate or compare, but it's natural human instinct to look upon others and see what you once had or may even want. I guess getting sick, having a dysfunctional marriage, losing my career, and dealing with raising a young Black man has gotten the best on me. I applaud my fellow sisters, but I'm dealing with some deep issues and don't need to be reminded about how successful that so-called friend is every time she calls. It's crazy how, when I say how I feel about my situation and get down in my dumps, she is quick to hang up the phone or has to go do something. I guess that call was only for her to bask in her glory and make herself feel good. Just a reminder that no one has time for people with problems or issues. Oh well, I didn't feel bad because my life hit a slump physically and financially. I continued to be the same caring loving giving friend for those in need for my life is not mine, but I am being used by the Lord.

I read a quote online that said, "Some people only check up on you to see if you have failed yet." Make sure you give a status report full of successes.

Brothers/Males Friends:

I get along with men better! Women are too chatty and our insecurities prevent us from accepting one another with love and open arms, all while uplifting one another. So, back to the brothers in my life. They are always accessible, they keep it real, and offer me the best advice. They are not judgmental, definitely do not compete with me, and they are superior Alpha men holding their own and living as kings.

A few of my bros are fine as wine and have conversations that peak my intellectual stimulus. Hey, I will never shoot my shot due to the fear of rejection. I'm human and still working on a few things, so don't judge me. It's like Erika Badu's "Next Lifetime" song. No I will not disclose them, but they know.

Although these categories of friends seem to meet all of my needs, my true friend is in the Lord. People will turn on you and treat you in ways that you did not think was imaginable, but hold fast to the Lord as God will never leave you or forsake you.

I find myself being a better friend to others than so-called friends are to me. I call friends, send care packages when they are sick, drop a text to check in and say hi, but I get nothing in return. I'm speaking for the majority, as I have a few friends that I speak with periodically. You know how everyone wants that BFF to share secrets, shop, laugh, travel with. Yeah, I don't have that friend so I decided to kick it solo. I have a better time with myself without drama, but I must admit it does get lonely always experiencing life and venturing out alone.

Just a thank you to those true friends that do call and check in on me. I do appreciate you and understand that you have busy lives and issues as well. And to the friends that I have wronged, I give my apologies again but I will never ever in dear life and beyond kiss an ASS to say that we are still cool. Let's be real. In all situations, good or bad, you learn a person's true character, how they respond, and their ability to move forward and carry on given a disagreement or argument.

All that being said, I know people are people, no more no less, and God will always be God.

Life Lessons:

Being the friend that I want and need makes me feel happy and serene. I no longer worry about the type of friends that I have but worry about the friend I want to be. Instead of building a brick wall, isolating myself, and being lonely, I have learned to meet people where they are and accept them for what they bring to the table.

Ask yourself how many Frenemies do you have? What category do the people you know fit into your life? Be prepared to let go and let God, as people will change for the reason and the season.

Tell people: Accept me for who I am. Love me for who I aspire to be. Help me when I am down. Believe in me when I don't believe in myself. And forgive me as I am not perfect.

The best advice that I have learned and given when dealing with others is to understand that person at their core and tailor your interaction and treatment accordingly.

SELF-RECOGNITION

In order to evolve as a person, one must first understand who they are. So my first name is Jo Anna and my middle name is Boshana. I always questioned my mom on why would she give me such an ethnically unique middle name. She often blamed it on my dad, while saying they were playing the alphabet game. Jo Anna, Boana, Fi, Phi, Fo, Fum Boshana. I was constantly teased and bullied about my middle name. Children can be so mean and cruel. They said things to make me feel embarrassed to tell my whole name and even made me feel bad about using my name outside of family. At the age of 34, I finally understood my middle name. I corrected the spelling to Boshana per my birth certificate and accepted that Boshana is who I am at the core. I no loner hide it. When people ask what does that mean or where does it come from, I tell the rhyming game from my father, but I also enlighten them to what it means to me and this name summed of my existence precisely.

Be.Original.Simple.Humble.Agile.Never.Apologetic

I am who I am, and I have nothing more to prove! I have finally recognized myself and my purpose on this earth.

Be Original:

We are created unique and different. Science has proven that there is not one identical person via our unique DNA. Being original is a part of who we are. We must learn to embrace our inner core and celebrate who we are in a world that tries to define beauty, prestige, and success.

Simple & Humble:

Sometimes we do too much as people to make ourselves into something that we are not instead of being simple and identifying the style, circumstance, and position that fits our character and spirit. On the other hand, once we reach our goals we forget where we come from and look down on our history and past, which may be someone's present state. As we develop, grow, and prosper, we must remember to be simple and humble as we are all human and can only be judged by God.

Agile:

You must figure out how to make things work, and how to maneuver through difficult situations and times. Nothing in life is perfect and adversity will exist in anything that you attempt. By developing the willingness and openness to learn and build upon the unknown, agility will manifest.

Never Apologetic:

Never apologize for being yourself. Stand fast in up-lifting your values and morals. Never apologizing does not mean committing unchristian acts and walking away. It simply means to have high self-confidence and esteem to pursue your dream, make tough decisions, and own who you are.

I found my way out, from self-hate to happiness. I will never change my name. I shorten it and use nick-names based on my relationship with people, but my given name is my name and I will never hide from it.

Life Lessons:

Stay in your lane, please. Do not try to be like every-one else. Discover your why for your own being and manifest in that. You will live a happy and prosperous life.

- Self-Awareness - Know who you are. No one will ever know you better than yourself. Be honest in the process of getting to know you and most definitely get comfortable.

- Self-Love - No one on earth can love you more than yourself. Show yourself daily love and ad-miration. You only have one life, as we know it, so make the best of it.

- Self-Happiness - Materials cannot make you happy. Learn early that happiness is a self-choice, and don't let the worldly trends and people impact your level of happiness.

You get it now? It's posted all over social media and these at home YouTube motivational speakers. People, especially women, are now focused on self-love. Don't stress about it. Take baby steps, and find out how to love yourself and keep building upon you! Remember, Rome was not built in a day, so don't be defeated. Come up with a plan, set quick wins, and stay focused to achieve the goals.

THE COVER UP

To adequately explain why I am referring to my life story thus far as a cover up, we must examine the definition of camouflage that is used in military environments to provide concealment and protection to soldiers.

According to dictionary.com, the definition of camouflage is:

verb (used with object), camouflaged, camouflaging.
to disguise by means of camouflage:
Synonyms: hide, conceal, mask, deceive, trick, dissimulate, dissemble.

To protect myself, I used various things to camouflage insecurities, pain, and fear. My whole life has been a cover up. I never really loved myself until now. I know it sounds crazy, but no matter what was seen on the outside, it never covered up the person that was the real me on the inside. It all makes sense now. I hid from myself, hence this book unveils my "cover up".

Throughout my life I used cover ups to protect me from my surroundings and feelings. I have never used any form of drugs in my entire life, but I have formed addictions to help me cover up the person I was on the outside to cope with the person who I had developed into on the inside. I pray and I know that I can see myself now.

Education:

The best cover up, I must say. School allowed me to hide from my past, conceal, my present, and focus on the future. I never wanted to focus on my current circumstances. I only looked forward. This allowed me to set goals and pursue my dreams, but I failed at life in its presence. I thought education was the answer. I was partially right. Knowledge will give you power, but you must learn how to use your power to elevate and enjoy life. Going to school, seeking higher knowledge, and obtaining certifications and licenses allows me to pursue interests and provide for myself and son.

Makeup:

I have suffered from acne since my teenage years. Originally onset by puberty and then again with the child bearing of my son, it's now a part of my life due to stress. I have tried everything under the sun to control my breakouts. Now it's about staying Zen and reducing my stress. I'm learning to fight the battles that are necessary vs. tackling every situation that comes my way. I am also learning that it is okay to take a break! Zone out and only focus on me.

Wigs:

A woman losing her hair is like the apocalypse. I am serious. If you are a woman, can you imagine losing your hair staring at the age of 19? Yes, 19. I was in college, and I started to develop a small bald patch at the top of my head. At first I thought it was due to chemical perms and even hot curling irons as I wore a short pixie, but now I know it was all due to stress. The stress of my childhood, family, troubled marriage, overbearing jobs, mother's illness, and eventually carrying my son.

Over a 6-year period my patch grew larger, and I could no longer hide it. I saw a dermatologist who gave me creams to use and even received steroid injections. All to fail and have continued hair loss.

Alopecia ran in the family, on both my maternal and fraternal sides. My great grandmother, grandmother, mother, and cousins all had it. I grew up watching them cover their baldness with wigs and hair extensions. I prayed it would skip me. Well, it didn't. Stylists and doctors blamed it on curling irons and chemicals, but I knew exactly what it was: Alopecia.

My mother had told me stories of how she lost her hair at the age of twelve, and that's why it was so thin later in life. I listened to her morn, telling hurtful stories of her hair loss. I encouraged her by speaking of her beauty and worth. She began to do the same for me as we learned to love ourselves together and embrace our beauty inside and out.

Materials:

Those that know me know I love to shop until I drop. I love fashion and the ability to illustrate my personality with clothes, shoes, and accessories.

When people saw my car, I wanted them to say, "Yeah, she doing it". No matter if I had a car that was completely paid for in full or a hefty car note, the vehicle I drove was definitely a status symbol that I used to and for others to define me.

Fancy materials are nice, but what about me? I spent my entire life worried about who I didn't want to be, and I began to bury myself in an image that I wanted to portray. When people looked at me, I wanted them to see beauty, grace, and quality. I began to shop! That's all I did. I wanted to cover up the pain from my childhood, the broken relationships, and the stress of life. Now that my mother and favorite cheerleader is no longer here with me, I must continue to love myself first and focus on my happiness as she constantly told and showed me.

The cover up is real, and it's okay for me to put on makeup and a wig from time to time. I love fashion and nice things, so I will spoil myself as well but the goal is to like and love the skin that I am in from the inside out. I like what we all consider the finer things in life and I will continue to place myself in situations to acquire them without dependence for love or attention. If you know me somewhat from what you have read in this book, you know that I will always entertain a learning opportunity throughout my life and experiences. I am not necessarily a new person, but I am no longer hiding behind the material and physical cover ups. I stand proud, confident, and transparent. I use materials as accessories to compliment the blessed woman that I am.

Life Lessons:

All my life I have been angry and mad, trying to find a way to cover it up instead of dealing with my problems. The daily task is to address the issues that you may have and find a comfortable resolution that will supersede a false cover up.

Love yourself first. Always make time for what is important to you, as you are the source of your happiness. Materials are not what makes you happy but the independence and ability to obtain those items is the joy.

In order to move forward with my life, I performed a self-inventory. I asked myself what am I good at.

- Solving problems.
- Helping others.
- Planning.
- Reaching people.
- I then asked myself what I like to do.
- Help others that want more.
- Show people my mistakes failures and bounce back to inspire them in their own lives.
- Organize and simplify.
- Sharing and caring.

I used these answers to develop goals that will make me happy and result in accomplishing ongoing happiness. I am not going to lie. I still have what I have defined as cover up issues. I still get overly stimulated aka excited at times when I'm angry, but I now know who I am. I try to de-escalate my zero to one hundred temper, and I'm working every damn day to be a better person. The person God intended me to be. Yes, I am working on my potty mouth. I understand that I am only human, but the difference now is that I am out of denial and on the glorious road to living within my purpose.

Each individual goal should be to love yourself and live abundantly. The problems come in to play when we start comparing ourselves to others. We should always remember to realign our happiness by focusing on ourselves, goals, and inner self in order to find self-love and peace.

Don't try to be perfect for the world. There is no such thing as perfection. The key is to realize that you can only be perfect for yourself. Embrace and enhance the flaws to find self-love in being different. I am saying that perfection is a level of self-comfort and confidence that can only be defined by an individual. Allow the cover ups to assist you yet not define you.

Lastly, stop doubting yourself and thinking that you are not good enough. Find self-confidence and build upon it. Help others to do the same and share love constantly. Remain humble and tactful when showing others that you encounter how to love themselves the same. The beauty of life is that nothing lasts forever, so it is wise to find a way to enjoy being yourself at all times. God will test you over again in certain situations if you don't learn the lesson or get the point, so it may seem as though you are constantly in the same rut. Note to self: open your eyes and see what God is trying to show you so that you can move forward with a happy life.

BEING BASIC JO

Now that the cover ups have been unveiled, I have to stop and think why am I still searching for love and dealing with hurt. I have so much to offer the world. I have worked at so many awesome places. I have traveled and lived in so many cool cities that people only dream of, but now what?

Recently, life has thrown me a barrel of sour lemons. Over the years I have learned to live and cherish everyday and use what I have to sweeten the lemonade by loving myself. As I have walked you through my motivational life story in this book, you can probably see that at this point in my life I am comfortable with being basically myself. For example, I have learned to deal with my chronic illness by embracing the "right now." I have learned to make concessions on things that tire me for opportunities to partake in activities that I enjoy the most. I have faced the tough facts that I can no longer put on my super mom cape and do it all by myself. I have acquired resources and help as needed. I am not going to lie: It is a process, and I have to mange each day differently. Upon waking up, I scan my physical and mental state so that I can determine what that day's agenda will realistically bring despite my tactical strategic plans. This is my daily start to being mindful and self-aware. I have stopped blaming myself for what I am no longer able to do, and I'm trying not to apologize with explanations. Because I love me, I can accept my imperfections and focus on what I can do for myself, son, and other loved ones.

Since my onset disabling illness, I've had to dig deep fighting pity and depression to recreate myself. With the leadership from my son, he told me who I ultimately needed to become based on how he perceived me. Because he saw me always talking to people, making new acquaintances, and illustrating joy, he coined me Network JO. He said to me, "Mom, you never met a stranger that you didn't know." I laughed and laughed. Then he said, "No Mom, I'm serious. You should be Network JO", after a discussion about my passion. I am now focusing on physical rehabilitation and learning how to manage my chronic pain.

After staying the dumps about my early onset illness, I dug myself out a deep, dark hole. I'm not trying to paint a pretty picture at all. I mean, I was in a deep depression, my marriage was over, career gone, and money exhausted. I slept for days without leaving the bed. Additional side effects started happening due to my high stress and withdrawal. I noticed my son's grades started slipping in school, and he was eating street food everyday. I was gaining weight. My skin was horrible; adult acne and life had taken over. When I saw that my son was being impacted by my slack in motherhood, I had to snap out of the depression. I called my mom and a close friend and let it all out. I talked about my darkest secrets and how I needed help to move forward. I got the support I needed, and I am learning to be optimistic about my new life.

You may be starting to ask, "So what's next?"

My mother always knew what to do and say to me to help me pick up the pieces and motivate me to reach my ultimate potential. I have taken years of my cover up and professional experience, and now I am ready to offer my knowledge to help people in my community who want more out of life. So, here's the potential pitch:

After 18 years in corporate America, I have decided to pursue a career in just simply being myself. I take pleasure in meeting new people, making connections, and building new relationships. I also love sharing information to help people achieve their goals or solve problems. Because of my passion for getting to know people, I am "Network JO". With this new brand, my goal is to share my knowledge of business, leadership, communication, and mentoring to those in need. This positive and motivated mindset will enable me to share my blessings with others as I address my medical needs.

Simply stated, I would eventually like to Educate, Motivate, and Coach!

Network JO will provide education, training, and development opportunities to all. We firmly believe that the key to success starts with a plan coupled with knowledge.

- At Network JO, all clients are inspired to set smart goals and make a plan to achieve them.

- Sometimes we become complacent and stop pursuing our dreams. Network JO provides accountability and an atmosphere for like minds to stay motivated and encouraged.

- At a time when there are limited resources and opportunities to learn from others, Network JO provides a plethora of coaches and mentors who can reach the client and achieve the Network JO mission.

Not to toot my own horn, but my stellar education and renowned work experience gives me a solid knowledge base to build upon. I can offer potential clients insight to their business, professional, and personal enrichment. I just want to create a platform that will help people that want more out of their businesses, careers, and lives.

Stay tuned as I streamline this concept by Being Basic JO.

Life Lessons:

Pursue your dreams and passions. Never accept no for an answer. Find out the reasons behind the no and pursue alternative solutions to acquire the yes you are seeking. Dream, build, and explore.

Be the reason you don't give up on yourself. Keep pushing through the hard times no matter what; you will prevail.

Hold your head up high. Nothing can break you. Nothing can stop you. He is only a man. He cannot determine your destiny. You have a blessed life and blessed opportunities that give you so much to look forward to. Love yourself and trust that God will help you through your struggle or bad situation. Also seek love and support from those who do care about you. You must carry on and seek resources so that you can reach your maximum potential to live an abundant life.

Find a way to express yourself by writing, blogging, painting, drawing, or any other hobby of your interest. Do the things that make you happy, and you will enjoy life.

Trust in a higher power to find clarity and vision. I can attest that nothing but my faith and the love of God keeps me going.

My son took a picture after my last surgery and showed me months later. He had placed a bouquet of flowers on me while I was sleeping. All I could think of when he showed me this was, *OMG what if I was dead*. I began to think: What if he was scared? At that point I knew that I had to keep fighting because I don't want him to see or remember me like the picture. I want him to always envision me as a fighter who never gave up. I want him to see me as a God-fearing believer who seeks strength from the Lord until my last days. From the day I saw the picture forward, I get up everyday to serve as a vessel for God's will be done and my body will be healed. This is the last lesson my mother taught me from her hospice bed, and I will continue to live my life with love as a servant of the Lord.

JO'ISMs

When coaching, mentoring, and even parenting, I tend to say some of the darnedest yet dope things. Here are some of my favorites that I use to motivate, teach, and inspire.

"When a person speaks, they may not be heard because they may not be saying anything worth listening to."

"Be mindful of who you are talking to and always meet people where they are at."

"Life hurts, but unfortunately you must endure the pain to see what God has in store for you."

"To my son, all I have to give you is knowledge; knowledge is power and no one can ever take it from you."

"There is nothing on earth that can't be replaced, except for life. Cherish every moment, dig deeper, and never forget your worth."

"Stepping out on faith, exposing your true self, and letting others see and feel the real you is the only thing that will make you comfortable in your own skin. Don't cover up! Nanny used to say, "Take off the slick coat and get real".

"The only way I can protect you is to give you knowledge. My grandfather always said, 'Learn what I know'. I get it Papa."

"We are all hurt and broken, but the ability to pick ourselves up and rebuild is what makes us strong and continues to give us strength to keep fighting."

"I don't know it all, but I try to learn something new everyday."

"When a person has dreams and goals that you don't understand or agree with, don't knock them down for their passion, yet help them figure out a way to achieve their mission. You will be showered with abundance and blessings beyond measure."

"If you throw out the trash, let it stay out. No need to keep trying to put the trash out. Moral is learn to let go.

It's hard, but the only way to achieve tranquility, bliss, and happiness."

"My sacrifices have created your inherited privileges. Embrace them with honor and pride. Now go out there, live, share, inspire, and teach others."

"It's always a way. It's never the end. Find the solution, and come up with the strategy. But you must work the system and never let it work you."

"Life is what you make it so take it."

ACKNOWLEDGE-MENTS

Dear God,

First and foremost, without you none of this would be possible. I give you, dear God, all the glory and praise for creating me, teaching me, and loving me unconditionally. Let your will be done with me as I give myself to you to use me.

I can accept me for who I am. Love me for who I aspire to be. Constantly seek guidance when I'm lost and help me when I am down. You believe in me when I don't believe in myself, and I love you for that constant encouragement. Please forgive me as I am not perfect, but I am a believer who is faithful.

-Amen

Jo Anna B. Thomas

Son,

This book would not be complete without me sprinkling some love over my son. Since July 17, 2005, you have become my everything. You have inspired me to keep going when the world shuts its doors in my face. You have moved around the country and traveled to lavish international destinations with me, taking on every situation as a fresh start and new life experience. You never complain about the racial disparity or racist encounters as I set out to do things differently and pursue the non-traditional African American corporate jobs at premier organizations.

Through every challenge and obstacle, I apologized for our instability but assured you that these experiences will set you apart from your peers and help mold you into the intelligent well-versed young brother that you are! I enjoy our "Mommy and the baby time." Yes, I just told the world you're my baby and I came up with that slogan and song for you to comfort and console you when you are down, by letting you know that I will always be with you on earth and I pray in heaven. Although I don't sing or say it often, I think our daily talks or brunch dates more than suffice and give us our time to bond.

Even though you are in the age frame where you think that you know more than I do, I cherish your dominance and independence as a young Black brother. I encourage you to never lose your voice. This is your gift from God and it is powerful, therefore you must be cautious and use it wisely. God has also placed you as angel in my life. Thank you for constantly following my lead and adapting to change. You push me to never give up and love myself as I have no choice but to provide you with love and the best example of parenthood.

I am often hard on you and expose you to real world conversations because I want you to be aware and prepared. With knowledge you will be able to analyze people and situations and make educated decisions as you conquer your dreams.

You may think that this is about me and my accomplishments, but it's really for you to learn from my failures. I know that you are only 11 years old, but I have so much to share with you. You made my heart smile when you told me, "Mom you have taught me enough life lessons to last 3-4 lifetimes." Now you must not forget them all, "Mr. smarty pants." LOL

I want you to understand why I love you so much and why I want you to love yourself even more. You must be aware that it is very important to be yourself and never hide who you truly are no matter what. By embracing your core, you will grow with confidence and power that cannot be bought or taught.

You must trust God and always remember it's God's plan, so live in God's will.

Always remember that knowledge is power and no one can ever take what you know from you. This book is definitely not your life guide but my testimony of God's saving grace that allowed me to stop covering up and fulfill the plan set for me. Use this book as a reminder and keep marching on through the turmoils that life can bring.

Parents always tell their children to be better than them, but I am telling you to be the best that you can be. Try to put your best foot forward in what you decide your goals and dreams are. This is a cruel world that we live in, and I want you to be prepared. This is why I tell you the real deal about everything. Sometimes it may come off a bit mean and I say things in raw form, but please know that I love you!

I'm so honest with you because the world will never be honest with you. Embrace your talents as a leader and effective communicator. Never let anyone or anything change who you are.

You are such an amazing young man! I love the person you are! People always ask me what I have done to raise you into the young man that you are, and I candidly tell them that I have done nothing but love you with all my heart. You are a blessed child of God. Continue to pray for guidance and forgiveness, as you will always need God's grace and anointing.

I want to thank you, my son, for being my reason to live and keep fighting. Mommy loves you with all of her heart and prays for blessings and love over your life. Thanks for branding me Network Jo and pushing me to keep going when I wanted to give up. I pray you accept my gifts of knowledge and wisdom as you grow up into an exquisite man.

I pray that one day you are able to sit down and write your story to inspire others and leave your family a legacy to build upon.

As you read along, I want you to continue to take on my good qualities of speaking up, fighting for what's right, changing what's wrong, and always helping others. That makes me sound like an angel, NOT. I want you to pay more attention to my fallacies as you learn more about my life in this book. I have always been honest and shared with you my issues, but I want you to dig deeper into my life story and truly understand me for who I am.

Love,

Momma

Momma,

You are no longer here with me to keep pushing me to achieve my goals, but you made it clear to me, before you left here, what to continue to focus on in life. You are my everything, and I will continue to make you proud so that you can have plenty to brag to your friends and family in heaven. I appreciate you so much. You told me that when you where no longer here, I would be able to finish this book as you were the last part of this chapter of my life and you were right. I am thinking clearer, and I have the freedom and confidence that you instilled in me. While taking care of you I learned so much about being a woman, mother, and daughter. I fussed, cleaned, and cooked but I listened to you, watched your expression, and learned your final ways. I am a stronger person, and I have a fraction of your wisdom to carry on as I work towards my personal goals and continue to raise you grandson.

In your final days I asked your advice on mother-hood, and you kept responding for me to love myself. I asked you several times, and I think I was getting in your nerves, but I thought you would have more to say until today as you are gone I stand firm on loving my-self first and it is strengthening me to be the best mom I can be. I am so grateful to have a mother like you.

You told me to always keep it real and tell others how I feel.

You gave me your smile and your style.

You encouraged all my dreams and told me to wear your name proudly.

You bulldozed all roadblocks for me so now I have no concept of constraints;

I only see endless possibilities.

When they said I was too fast you told them to kiss your bottom, because you knew I was a smart little girl just like you were that just needed some love and attention.

We fussed with each other about a lot of things, but that was our way of pushing each other to be at our best.

It will always be Mommy & Me.

Since day one, we could never be apart.

The nurses tried to feed me, but I would not eat,

All I wanted was to be with my mommy.

Things haven't changed since.

I never left your side.

There has not been a place where I have not followed.

I insisted that you take my everywhere with you.

Even when you left me at home,

I managed to find my way to my mommy!

As you pursued higher education in college I followed you to school, at Olive Harvey, Kennedy King, and the Neighborhood Institute.

You worked hard on multiple jobs to pave the way as a single mother with two children, and I tried to help you so I followed you to work at Dominick's, Ma & Pa Food and Liquors, Marvin's Onyx, Steve's Food, and Starbucks. Whether it was bagging groceries, making lists, or getting whatever you needed, I stood by your side to help in anyway that I could.

I love you so much that I celebrated life with you, and I insisted on being a part of your happiness so I eased my way to parties at your friends homes and gatherings. I just always wanted to be with you because you were all that I had and the only love I received came directly from you.

Even in times of disparity, homelessness, sickness, and instability, I have never left your side. When I was a child you led the way exemplifying courage, strength, and agility. This has made me into the woman I am today. I appreciate you and continue to follow your lead.

As you consistently exclaim:

"I been there and done that"

My mommy you are always there when I need you.

I can count on you to be right here by my side at the drop of dime.

Even when I upset you, you still answer my calls no matter what.

"Mommy, can you ... Mommy, will you ...

Mommy, please... Mommy, I will pay you back...

Mommy, I love you..."

Anywhere I go, or anything I do, I will always have a part of you mommy with me! As you laid in that hospice bed I often chanted to myself.

MY BEST FRIEND

MY FAMILY

MY HEART

MY SOUL

MY INSPIRATION AND DEDICATION

MY MOMMA IS MY EVERYTHING

YOU ONLY REALIZE WHAT YOU HAVE

BUT YOU REALLY DO NOT UNDERSTAND YOUR LOVE

UNITL IT IS AT RISK OF BEING TAKEN AWAY FROM YOU.

I CALL HER MY PRETTY

NOT BECAUSE OF HER PROFOUND LOOKS AND BEAUTIFUL SMILE

BUT BECAUSE OF HER GIVING SPIRIT AND LOVING HEART

SHE GAVE ME AND MY BROTHER HER ALL AND SHE BECAME

MY PRETTY

Everyday we said goodnight as I said Mommy I love you, while you said

Shana I love you more, and we concluded simultaneously with the powerful love filled word of Impossible.

Here is my tribute to you:

I promise to continue to educate myself and ensure my son has the same opportunities that you afforded me to learn and seek knowledge. I continue to be Dora and explore this world, finding peace and serenity. I will place myself first in all prioritization and love me for the beautiful intelligent woman that I am. In this process of enjoying life and living, I will be able to find someone to love me the way that I want to be loved. This is all my way of taking care of myself and continuing your elegant and graceful legacy.

Love,

Shana

Divine Legacy
PUBLISHING, LLC.

Creative Control With Self-Publishing

Divine Legacy Publishing provides authors with the guid-ance necessary to take creative control of their work through self-publishing. We provide:

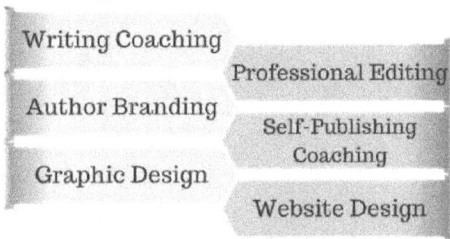

- Writing Coaching
- Professional Editing
- Author Branding
- Self-Publishing Coaching
- Graphic Design
- Website Design

Let Divine Legacy Publishing help you master the business of self-publishing.

www.ingramcontent.com/pod-product-compliance
Lightning Source LLC
Chambersburg PA
CBHW031539040426
42445CB00010B/606